CAMBRIDGE LIBRARY COLLECTION

Books of enduring scholarly value

Women's Writing

The later twentieth century saw a huge wave of academic interest in women's writing, which led to the rediscovery of neglected works from a wide range of genres, periods and languages. Many books that were immensely popular and influential in their own day are now studied again, both for their own sake and for what they reveal about the social, political and cultural conditions of their time. A pioneering resource in this area is Orlando: Women's Writing in the British Isles from the Beginnings to the Present (http://orlando.cambridge.org), which provides entries on authors' lives and writing careers, contextual material, timelines, sets of internal links, and bibliographies. Its editors have made a major contribution to the selection of the works reissued in this series within the Cambridge Library Collection, which focuses on non-fiction publications by women on a wide range of subjects from astronomy to biography, music to political economy, and education to prison reform.

Writings on Education in West Africa

Hannah Kilham (1774–1832) was a missionary whose aim in her work in the Gambia and Sierra Leone was to teach children in their own indigenous languages rather than in English. In order to do so she learned the Wolof language from African sailors in London and later, in Sierra Leone, collected specimens of thirty languages through her encounters with freed slaves. The first of two short publications reissued in this volume, Kilham's *Report on a Recent Visit to the Colony of Sierra Leone* (1828), discusses the state of education in the colony as well as the general condition of its people, their health, and their dwellings. The second text, *Claims of West Africa to Christian Instruction through the Native Languages* (1830) also discusses the system of education, outlining the process of tuition, and emphasising the need for Bible translations into African languages. For more information on this author, see http://orlando.cambridge.org/public/svPeople?person_id=kilhha

T0371215

Cambridge University Press has long been a pioneer in the reissuing of out-of-print titles from its own backlist, producing digital reprints of books that are still sought after by scholars and students but could not be reprinted economically using traditional technology. The Cambridge Library Collection extends this activity to a wider range of books which are still of importance to researchers and professionals, either for the source material they contain, or as landmarks in the history of their academic discipline.

Drawing from the world-renowned collections in the Cambridge University Library, and guided by the advice of experts in each subject area, Cambridge University Press is using state-of-the-art scanning machines in its own Printing House to capture the content of each book selected for inclusion. The files are processed to give a consistently clear, crisp image, and the books finished to the high quality standard for which the Press is recognised around the world. The latest print-on-demand technology ensures that the books will remain available indefinitely, and that orders for single or multiple copies can quickly be supplied.

The Cambridge Library Collection will bring back to life books of enduring scholarly value (including out-of-copyright works originally issued by other publishers) across a wide range of disciplines in the humanities and social sciences and in science and technology.

Writings
on Education
in West Africa

Hannah Kilham

CAMBRIDGE UNIVERSITY PRESS

Cambridge, New York, Melbourne, Madrid, Cape Town, Singapore,
São Paolo, Delhi, Dubai, Tokyo, Mexico City

Published in the United States of America by Cambridge University Press, New York

www.cambridge.org
Information on this title: www.cambridge.org/9781108019149

© in this compilation Cambridge University Press 2010

This edition first published 1828-30
This digitally printed version 2010

ISBN 978-1-108-01914-9 Paperback

REPORT

ON

A RECENT VISIT TO THE COLONY

OF

SIERRA LEONE.

BY

HANNAH KILHAM.

LONDON:

PRINTED BY WILLIAM PHILLIPS, GEORGE-YARD LOMBARD-STREET;
SOLD BY HARVEY AND DARTON, GRACECHURCH-STREET;
AND EDMUND FRY, HOUNDSDITCH.

1828.

To the Committee for African Instruction, and other Friends concerned in promoting its objects.

—◆◆—

ALTHOUGH gratefully sensible of the obligations under which I am placed toward Friends, who have kindly favoured my desire to visit the Coast of Africa, I yet feel so deeply impressed with the conviction that the *cause itself* only, is worthy of notice in this Report, that most gladly would I lose sight of my own individual engagement in it, only to acknowledge that Infinite Mercy, by which an unworthy servant has been protected and sustained: preserved and restored from sickness by land, and delivered from the dangers of an awful storm at sea, when the waves seemed ready to overwhelm, and ourselves as at the very gate of death. And thankfully would I acknowledge also, the deep sense with which my mind has been impressed, of the little moment of all transitory sufferings or enjoyments, in comparison of the concerns which we shall feel to be of everlasting interest, in that swiftly approaching hour when we shall each have to stand as alone before our Judge.

We were favoured, after a rapid passage to Sierra Leone, with a safe and pleasant landing, on First day morning, the 9th of 12th month, 1827.

In anchoring at this Port, the fine open view of Free Town, in which are many handsome buildings,

the fresh and beautiful foliage of trees in its vicinity,
and the mountains covered with verdure, rising in ma-
jestic grandeur in the bounds of our view, presented a
scene so interesting, that, together with the attraction
felt towards the dear children on the coast, it was not
easy to imagine there could be any *unconquerable*
difficulty as to European residence in the country ;
still it could not be concealed from the most sanguine,
that, even in *approaching* these shores, the influence of
the heat was felt to be greatly relaxing, and experience
must confirm the conviction of the precariousness of
European life on this coast, and of the great claim
which the instruction of Native Teachers presents, for
the prompt and efficient help of the friends of Africa.

It was a great comfort to us soon to meet some of
our dear friends on shore. Several of the Missionaries
had been seriously ill during the rains (which had ceased
only three weeks) but they were now recovered, excepting one who was still sick at Wellington. With some
of the Missionaries I had been previously acquainted
in England, and with others had had the advantage of
friendly open communication on the way, on subjects
of importance, and of mutual interest. My kind friends
J. and A. Weeks, invited me immediately to take up
my abode with them : (A. W. I had previously known
in Africa and in England). Although their hospitality
and friendship in this distant land were truly consoling, and I felt it as a claim for thankfulness to Him,
who is present to help and protect as well when far off
from near relatives and home, as in any other circumstances, yet I could not at once conclude upon any
thing more than to remain with them for the present,
and wait to see whether Free Town or the village districts, would be most favourable for pursuing the
objects in view.

On the day after our landing I visited the Free Town Eastern School, which, since the removal of a number of the Free Town children to this school, in the early part of last year, had been conducted by J. and A. Weeks, with two Native Assistants. The school contained about 200 Children, Boys on one side and Girls on the other, without farther division than a few slight posts, at a distance from each other. The room had been built for the purpose, ample and commodious, and very pleasantly situated near the sea. The scholars are chiefly the children of the American settlers, together with a few others sent fron Native districts in the vicinity of Sierra Leone, and boarded in Free Town at the expense of their parents, for the advantage of having them sent to the day schools.

The attention and intelligence of the Boys in this school delighted me ; and never did I see a company of children in any school whose countenances struck me as more expressive of a lively disposition to, imbibe instruction, and quick capacity for receiving it. They answered with readiness from the Scriptures, questions on many interesting and important subjects, and evidently enjoyed the opportunity given them of receiving farther instruction. The Girls joined in attending to the questions thus proposed by J. W. to the whole school, but, though the countenances of many of them were intelligent and interesting, they did not appear to have attained to the same scriptural knowledge with the Boys. They had, during the late rains, been under great disadvantages ; the almost constant sickness of A. W. preventing her being able to attend the school during a great part of the season.

There was another School for Boys and Girls in Free Town (now called the Western School) in which the number of Scholars was rather larger than in this.

The Boys taught by a Native Teacher and his Assistant, and the Girls by M. Taylor, the widow of a Missionary, and S. Fox, the wife of the Master of the Boys school, as her Assistant. Some changes have since taken place in the arrangement of the Schools, on account of the return of J. and A. Weeks to England, for the recovery of their health. No Europeans being at liberty to take charge of the school on their departure, the Boys of both schools were placed under the care of the Native Teacher, George Fox, who had his education in England, and the Girls under M. Taylor, with the Native Assistants in each school.

For several days during the school vacation, which commenced on the 15th, J. W. assembled a large company of little children, together with a number of the other scholars, to try the effect of some parts of the Infant School system, and with a success so interesting, that we could not but greatly desire such a school for the junior children could be formed in that place.

The engagements I had in view in Sierra Leone were, first, the obtaining an outline of the principal languages spoken by the Liberated Africans and others in the Colony, so as, by taking down in writing, in an easy and distinct orthography, the numerals and some of the leading words, to identify, so far as might be practicable, the dialects of the different tribes, to form an idea of the number of distinct languages spoken in Sierra Leone; and to consider what prospect there might be of proceeding to reduce those of most importance to a written form. Also to prepare such an outline for elementary instruction in each language, as might introduce the pupils in the Liberated African Schools, to a better knowledge of English than they at present possess.

From observations made in Sierra Leone, and from

subsequent reflection, it has appeared quite likely that this purpose may be effected, if the children can learn at first only fifty or sixty leading words, besides the numerals, each in their own language, and the correspondent words in English. This would indeed seem but as a small beginning, but so many leading words *attained* and *understood*, would soon introduce to an extension of their knowledge. At present the Liberated African children are learning English under the same disadvantages, which English children would have in learning French, were French books only given to them, without any English translation. The children in the villages have but little opportunity of hearing *conversation* in English, excepting in the barbarous broken form of it, which prevails in that district, and which consists of but a very limited number of words (some suppose not more than fifty) : the written language of their English books of course appears quite as a foreign tongue in comparison with this; therefore, although many learn in time to *read* and to *spell*, those who are thus circumstanced cannot be expected to *understand* what they read. The children of the Free Town schools have superior advantages in this respect—their parents being chiefly from the American Continent or Islands, they are brought up by them in *speaking* as well as reading the English language.

The School vacation in Free Town having commenced so soon after my arrival in Sierra Leone, my friends J. and A. Weeks, kindly accompanied me to several villages of Liberated Africans in pursuance of the objects in view. The first place which we visited was Wellington, of which Thomas Macfoy, a native of the West Indies, is Superintendant. From his Register of the names and native countries of the people under his care, I found an unexpected facility in obtaining a knowledge of how many tribes were resident in the village, and the number of persons belonging to each. From these various tribes T. Macfoy sent out for the most intelligent individuals as interpreters, yet in some instances it seemed necessary for himself or J. Weeks to act as an *intermediate interpreter*, for such of them as could not understand any other than the broken English. Besides Wellington, we visited in this engagement Allen's Town, Leopold, Regent, and Gloucester; and J. W. went alone to Charlotte, to ascertain whether any other tribes were to be met with there. Sketches were taken down of the numbers, and of some leading words in twenty-five languages, and J. W. suggested, that by an arrangement which would present at one view a few words in each language, one elementary book might serve for a whole school, although the children might be of many different tribes. The idea was adopted, and a manuscript was afterwards, during my passage home, arranged in that order. Two of the dialects taken down in the villages, had been omitted, as being too similar to some others, to be regarded as distinct; and three having been added in Free Town, the whole prepared for the proposed elementary book, including the Jalof, Mandingo, Timmani, and Sussu, previously printed, were thirty in number, and, with the addition of the English, they are now presented to the notice of the Committee, under the title of "Specimens of African Languages," &c.

In the "African School Tracts," which your Committee kindly printed last year, and which the Missionaries have concluded to adopt in the schools,* a

* Although the Village Schools, as part of the Liberated African department, are under the care and support of Government, the Church Missionary Society have still the charge of supplying them with books and other School apparatus.

short series of Elementary Spelling Lessons are given, in the same orthography with the " Specimens," and it is considered that when these two books have been learned by the children, they may proceed to the little Narratives in the School Tracts, and increase by degrees their knowledge of English.

For their better understanding English, a small and easy Dictionary appears to be still wanting, in which words of frequent and requisite use might be explained in a manner sufficiently clear and intelligible for these children, by using as much as possible in the explanations, only such words as are of the most obvious and tangible kind; such a little book might possibly be prepared for them in this country.

From all the Missionaries, I had the satisfaction of meeting with a very kind and friendly reception, and a ready concurrence with the views suggested as to elementary translations; it was however remarked by one, that should Slave Ships cease to be brought to this Colony, on account of the proposed arrangements respecting Fernando Po, the necessity for this work would in some respects diminish, as to the schools in Sierra Leone, although still useful to the present residents in the Colony. From this Missionary, T. Davy, and from another, W. K. Betts, I received material assistance, by their writing Vocabularies of the Aku* language, from the dictation of Natives, and furnishing me with a copy of what they had taken down. This language is said to be spoken by more than half the Liberated Africans in Sierra Leone, and on this account important to cultivate. In this language, and in the Bassa,

* Aku, the name used for this nation in the Colony, but it appears from their information that the name of their country is E-i-o, and the term Aku only their word of salutation in meeting.

which is spoken by many in Sierra Leone, and very generally in Liberia, larger Vocabularies have been taken than in any others, excepting the few which had been previously printed.

In addition to the preparation of elementary books, an object greatly desired was, that Schools under the care of Native Teachers should be formed, in some of the villages which had not yet come under the care of any Society for school instruction; and very soon after arriving in Sierra Leone, the way appeared plainly to open for this, by information from two devoted and exemplary men, Missionaries of the Wesleyan Methodist Society, who were much disposed to give their voluntary attention, by visiting schools, and saw them greatly wanted in two villages in their immediate vicinity, Portuguese Town and Kongo Town : but they were not commissioned by their friends to form such schools.

A few friends at Peckham, members of the Female Antislavery Association, with some others united with them, had commissioned me to see one Village School opened on an easy simple scale, and had sent a donation of ten guineas for this purpose, intending to continue it annually. Portuguese Town was fixed upon as the place most prep red for the commencement of a school, the parents there being anxious to have their children taught. The Wesleyan Missionaries judging it best to put the parents upon doing what they could for themselves, proposed that a small sum should be paid by them for each child : it was however found that these payments would not prove a sufficient supply for the salary of the native teacher, which required about £16 or £20 a year. This with the lessons, would be the whole expense of the school, the Missionaries having appropriated their chapel to be used in the day time as the school house. They wished to use as little of a voluntary fund as could be for the Portuguese Town School, and desired rather to devote a part to the commencement of another school, which was much wanted in Kongo Town, a place in which the people were so very poor, that they could not be expected to pay much, if any thing, themselves, for their children's instruction. Where this *can* be done—where parents can pay something themselves toward providing for a Native Teacher, it is greatly to be wished even on their own account, that they should thus act a Parent's part, and this subject I was anxious to press upon the attention of the people in Portuguese Town, in an opportunity for communication which I had with them in their own village, on the important and interesting duties of parents in the education of their children.

It was concluded before I left Sierra Leone, that a school should soon after that time be opened in Kongo Town, and our Peckham friends have since proposed not only to provide for the expenses of these two schools, but to take charge of another also if opened in Kroo Town, a village which being in the vicinity of Free Town, the school might be visited as the others by the Wesleyan Missionaries.

There are several villages not far from the settlements of liberated Africans, in which schools of this kind might be formed, and which are at present without any means of instruction.

In the Colony there are at present twenty-four schools in which Native Teachers are employed, besides the one now opened in Portuguese Town, and a small private school for little children in Free Town. Of the schools under the care of Government there are twenty, in which *only* Native Teachers are employed;

but the attainments of many of these are said to be very low. The Agents of Church Missionary Society are considered as having a general liberty to visit and direct the teachers in all the schools under the care of Government, but the number of Missionaries in the colony is at present very small, in proportion to the extent of ground they have to occupy, and the number of villages to be visited by them for religious instruction. In six of the school stations, children are received from the Slave Ships, and their board as well as schooling provided for. The others are Free Day Schools for the village children.

The scholars in these Village Day Schools are chiefly the children of liberated Africans, now settled in the different villages and providing for themselves. Most of them have some little spot of land in cultivation, which they call their farm, and on which they raise cassada and a few other vegetables, which to many families form their chief subsistence.

The new agricultural village, called Allen's Town, and another lately formed on the same principle, called Newlands, are both within two or three miles of Wellington, and under the superintendance also of T. Macfoy, with a submanager or Headman, resident in each. Allen's Town is beautifully situated on the road from Free Town by Kissey and Wellington, to the more distant villages of Hastings, Waterloo, Calmont, and Kent. The formation of this village has been commenced on a plan very favourable to agricultural occupation, the farms being in immediate connexion with the dwellings.

From the account received from T. Macfoy, respecting the people committed to his care from the Slave Ships, we learn that on their arrival, such as are tolerably healthy, are sent out in companies into the woods, under the care of some older resident, and thence bring materials to build their houses, which are made in a long square of tolerable size, two rooms on the floor, an opening in the form of window in each, a little depository in the roof for their stores, and in the front of the house a viranda, which, with the roof, is thatched with dried grass. Six or eight persons join in building one house, and then another, until all are provided. Little or no expense is incurred in building in this way, the materials being so near at hand. Allotments of land are laid out behind each house, and food raised upon them. For the first six months after their arrival in the Colony, each adult liberated African is allowed a little clothing, and 3d. per day to purchase food ; out of this I am informed many of them can keep a part for other purposes. At the end of six months this allowance ceases, as it is expected that they will then have cleared a little ground, and have begun to raise some provision for themselves.

Allen's Town, at the time of our visit, had not more than 25 dwelling houses finished ; these were chiefly inhabited by a company of about 50 persons, received not much more than a year since from the Slave Ships, and some of them in a weak and sickly state, not capable of much labour.

A number of Kosso families were coming into the village, and beginning to build, and settle among them. T. M. the superintendant, gives only a little land to the Kosso's, as they are generally an unsettled class of people, and often removing, but informs them, that if found industrious and steady, they shall have more land. Although the village is but lately commenced and small, a place conveniently situated for both the inhabitants and persons passing through, is set apart as a market, and shaded with a thatched roof.

A school house is built in the village ; the size 30 feet by 15. The master, a young man brought up in one of the Missionary Schools, had, when we saw the place, eighteen liberated African boys boarding with him, and a few village children as day scholars. They had several of them made very good progress in reading, although not yet twelve months under his care. The boarders have since been removed to another station, and the school continued for the children of the village only as day scholars.

In the vicinity of Allen's Town, I was told there is a fine station for an Agricultural School, in which pupils might be trained to field labours during a part of the day, and school instruction during another part. An intelligent, respectable, and religious man, an American of African descent, who has filled the offices of School Master and of Magistrate in Sierra Leone, would, if the way were quite open for it, gladly devote himself to the work of education, combined with agricultural engagements; and Maria Macfoy, who has had the advantage of education in America, would willingly take a few young girls into her family, to be brought up in industry and school instruction, with a view to their future usefulness as Teachers. In the present lack of Native Teachers, this appears an opening for both male and female instruction that claims attention.

The proposed situation offers peculiar facilities for a training establishment, and for doing much good, not only by preparing Native Teachers, but for the instruction of children from several neighbouring villages. The native villages of Robis, Ro - ku - pa, and Ro-bomp, are all near, and have not schools. Several kinds of produce for sale could, I am informed, be easily raised in this situation ; Cayenne pepper, ginger, arrow root, gum arabic, gum copal, coffee, and cotton.

The first wants of life are very easily supplied in Sierra Leone, and the people are much disposed to add to these, by the disposal of surplus produce, when they have the opportunity. They take great pains in bringing their little produce down from the villages to Free Town market ; and when they hear of provision being wanted in their own neighbourhood for the liberated African children, there are sometimes so many applications, that the Superintendant has a difficulty in satisfying his own feelings, by dividing the order, so as to allow a number of them to have each a share in the supply.

The Africans in the Colony of Sierra Leone, are acknowledged to be a docile, affectionate people, and easily governed ; but very serious difficulties are sometimes experienced in cases of trial before Magistrates, from the little knowledge the people have of the English language ; and to a feeling mind it must be found truly distressing when, as is sometimes the case in trials affecting life, it can hardly be distinguished, after a long and harrassing examination, who are the innocent, or who the guilty.

From the same deficiency, children in the schools have sometimes been punished for disobedience, when it has afterwards been found that they did not understand the command or direction given.

T. Macfoy experiences an evident advantage in the large village in which he lives, from classing his people according to their tribes, and placing one of the older residents of the same tribe over each company. These Overseers (who have the name of Constables) communicate with the people more fully and easily than T. Macfoy could do himself, knowing their language and

their habit of thought. They endeavour to settle for
them what are called " small palavers," or little difficulties and contests ; but subjects of more importance,
or any that they cannot satisfactorily settle, are brought
to T. M. as their Superintendant, to decide.

The good feeling which subsists between T. Macfoy
and the people under his care, is truly pleasant to
witness. Their conduct on one memorable occasion is
worthy to be recorded, as a striking proof of their
affectionate, courageous, and truly generous feeling,
in a moment of extreme danger. The store near to T.
Macfoy's house, had taken fire. It contained, among
other things, a barrel of gunpowder, which had been got
for blowing up rocks in making the new roads. T. M.
in his first alarm, called on the people to escape for
their lives, but they promptly replied, " No, no, we
must fight that powder;" and rushing by the flames,
they with a quick and laborious effort, disengaged the
barrel, and brought it out. Whilst T. M. was attending to the extinction of the flames, some of the people,
from the fear that the house might yet take fire, took
away his wife and children to convey them to a place
of safety. M. Macfoy had but lately been confined to
her room, and wept inanxiety and distress, as they
brought her away. They tried to comfort her, saying,
" Don't cry, Ma-my—your children shall *not* be lost
—your house shall *not* burn." T. M. returned to his
house, and found it stripped of his family, and of furniture, and knew not where they were gone. In going
out into the road, he saw there the furniture spread out
in a line, and menregularly placed along to guard it.
On the furniture being brought back, it appeared that
there was not any thing lost, and only a single glass
tumbler broken. T. Macfoy was affected with the con-

duct of the people, and speaking to them of what he felt towards them, and his wish that he could return their kindness, they quickly replied, that they wanted no return, but that which they now enjoyed.

From the report of the Liberated African School of Leopóld, printed last year, I was painfully struck with the proportion of deaths among the children, and with the number at that time sick. Observing that other schools had not made any point of reporting on the state of the children's health, I could not but feel it a matter of importance that such reports should be regularly required on behalf of all the liberated African children, both with respect to health, and to their state of instruction; and should it appear that there is more of sickness among these children, than even their debilitated state on arrival will account for, farther enquiry should undoubtedly be made as to the cause, or causes.

That some of these poor little children do appear on arrival only like moving skeletons, is indeed true. Nothing but the very representation of death, could equal the worn and wretchedly emaciated appearance, that some of these presented when I lately saw them, having but within a few weeks been received from the Slave Ship. There are sometimes melancholy instances of a feverish, ravenous appetite, inducing these miserable little victims of oppression, as soon as they land and are brought within sight of poultry and other kinds of food, to fall upon stealing it, half roasting if possible, and eagerly devouring it, yet still feeling always in want, and always out of health.

The breaking up of the schools of liberated African children some time ago, and their distribution as apprentices to such as would take them, is the more to be lamented, as there are not at present any means of collecting these children or ascertaining that they are well treated; some arrangement to bring them occasionally into view, is greatly wanted; some of the people who take them, after having paid ten shillings for an indenture, imagine that they have by this means purchased the children, and made them their own property.

The plan which had been previously pursued of collecting the children into schools on being landed from the Slave Ships, and providing for their board and instruction until they are of an age to support themselves, is now resumed with respect to the newly received children generally, but not so as to preclude some being put out as apprentices if wanted.

There is not I think a more promising appearance in any quarter with respect to African instruction, than the recent introduction by one of the Missionaries, Thomas Davy, on his return to Sierra Leone, of the Infant School system. The plan introduced by him at Leopold is indeed somewhat modified, and the exhilirating practices of some of the schools here, rather softened down, which for Africa is quite necessary; but it will probably require some further variations, or still remain rather too exhausting for a school to be wholly conducted by the same teacher.

The tangible and attractive nature of this system renders the instruction more intelligible to children who know but little English, than any that has yet been practised in Sierra Leone, and it has not been my lot to visit any infant school in England in which the system was acted upon with more interesting effect than in this at Leopold, which I trust may be presented as an example to the native teachers, and a model Infant School for Sierra Leone. The system addressing itself to the eye, as well as to the ear, the lessons become more easy to understand, than in the common mode of teaching; and the *kind, friendly* manner in which instruction is imparted, incites and cherishes the best feelings, and opens a way to the *hearts* of the dear little children when religious instruction is thus conveyed to them. The widow of Thomas Heighway, a kind-hearted, pious, and estimable woman, after the early removal of her beloved companion, who lived only a few weeks in the colony, believing it to be her religious duty to remain still in Africa, has taken the charge of this interesting school, at least for the present. Thomas Davy, at the time we left Sierra Leone, was about to give instruction in the system to Maria Macfoy, who wished to introduce it at Wellington. Some lessons and pictures which I had taken with me, would supply her school for the present. The Superintendant of the liberated African department had sent for several sets of apparatus from England, after seeing the School at Leopold.

It was intended, after visiting the villages, to have assembled the children in Free Town on a First-day afternoon for a little opportunity of religious instruction, adapted to their state and understandings. This proposal was agreed to by the conference of Missionaries, but sickness, and returning so soon after, prevented. I still hope that the subject may be considered, and that in Free Town particularly, where the children know the English language so much better than in the villages, a part of the day appropriated for religious engagements for the senior classes of society, may, by some affectionate and serious minded teachers be devoted to the religious instruction of those in the earlier stages of life, when the mind is most impressible.

The friends of the dear little children of Sierra Leone have had many and great difficulties to encounter in labouring in that station. May they not be discouraged, but supplicate for the favour and guidance of Him who only knoweth " the hearts of all the children of men," and can teach them in what way to endeavour to direct the minds of their interesting charge to their Creator and Redeemer; and make them instrumental through His divine favour and blessing in leading the dear children even in the very early stages of life to a real sense and feeling of that which is good.

C. F. Hainsel, with whom I had conversation respecting the formation of a library for the young people in Free Town, kindly engaged to see one put under suitable care, when it should be sent. Also small libraries for some of the villages, if books can be found sufficiently easy for the village districts. Some books which had been selected for a library, I thought it best to leave for C. F. H.'s boys, if approved by himself.

As there are not at present any school books or tracts to be *bought* in Sierra Leone, and some of the people in Free Town would gladly purchase them if they could obtain them, I suggested to C. F. H. that some might possibly be sent from an association in England on my return, on which he readily offered to place them for sale, if sent to his care, in the hands of a respectable American in Free Town. In this and other instances I felt grateful for his kind attention to several concerns which must depend on some one remaining in the Colony; but life is I am aware to all uncertain. C. F. Hainsel's prospect of conducting an establishment at Foura Bay for training Native Teachers, and his services in the Colony in other important directions, renders the continuance of his life greatly desirable, if so it may be permitted. It is hoped that information may from time to time be obtained from Sierra Leone as to the outlines of any new languages found there: but in order for a European to *proceed* much with the study of any of these languages, and to have the requisite aid in translation from the natives, it would be necessary that the natives to be thus employed, should have a knowledge of English beyond what can easily be obtained without a residence for a time in this country.

How much cause have I to look back with gratitude for the kindness with which my short visit to the Colony of Sierra Leone was received by the Missionaries and teachers there, and the Christian sympathy, friendship, and hospitality with which I was favoured.

In sickness and in health, I had from J. & A. Weeks the kind care of near relations. Their solicitude for me was still continued when we were all three confined with fever, and in separate apartments under the care of native nurses. I have indeed to acknowledge that nothing was lacking; and especially to remember with thankfulness the sustaining and consoling sense of Divine Goodness near, with which my mind was visited in the first attack of sickness, and the support still experienced in its continuance from the assurance that He would order " all things well," and all in mercy.

To Joseph Reffel, and to several of the Colonial residents, I had to acknowledge my obligation for their readiness to facilitate my engagements, and for other marks of friendly attention : and particularly the unremitting and judicious care of Dr. Boyle during my sickness, himself but just recovered from fever, I hope ever to retain in grateful recollection.

My mind has for years been impressed with a conviction, that our great duty toward Africa, is to strengthen the hands of the people, *to promote each other's good*; and, if we may be so permitted, to be instrumental in leading some to the acknowledgment of Christianity from experimental feeling, who may become humble instruments in the Divine hand of spreading the Truth and the love of it, and especially among the rising generation in Africa. It is the Africans themselves that must be the Travellers, and Instructors, and Improvers of Africa : — let Europeans aid them with Christian kindness, as senior brethren would the younger and feebler members of their Father's family— but let it be kept in mind to what perpetual interruption every purpose must be subject, that is made dependant upon European life on the African shores.

Let a full and fair opportunity be given, if by Divine favour and assistance it may be so permitted, for preparing Agents of intelligence and Christian feeling from among the Natives themselves. Let them be trained in habits which will lead them to the exercise of their own understanding, and let them be taught to make good use of their own resources, and not disposed to look to others to do for them, what is within their own power by proper exertion and attention, to do for themselves,—and, above all, may they be taught to feel and thankfully acknowledge, that their beneficient Creator, the Father of all the families of the earth, wills the happiness and redemption of all—that all mankind are indeed in a fallen state and prone to evil— but that the effects of our first Parents fall are not more universal, than the blessing of an universal opening to Redemption by Christ Jesus ;—that, a measure of His divine light and renewing power is imparted to "every man that cometh into the world," and would lead all if yielded to, to salvation, from sin and misery, and would conduct to final happiness :—but where men will "love darkness rather than light, because their deeds are evil," and "will not come unto the light, lest their deeds be reproved," then, although the light may still in degree continue to shine, its power and efficiency will not be felt ; it will shine only as on the darkness that " comprehendeth it not"—and the offers of mercy and redemption afforded, will, if thus slighted and neglected, rise up against them to their condemnation.

I left Sierra Leone, in company with my friends J. and A. Weeks, on the 20th of 2d month, and it seems due from me here to acknowledge, that soon after coming on board, I was favoured with a sense of the overshadowing of Divine care and goodness, so indubitable and consoling, that my mind was covered with thankfulness, and with a feeling of peace inexpressible.

Extract from Memorandums at Sea in returning home.

4th month 5th, 1828.

I feel thankful for the opportunity of visiting Sierra Leone, and have before I went the second time thought, that to be there only for *one month,* I could be glad to undertake the voyage. ...... My own mind, now so far divested of the concern as to be fully at liberty to pursue African and other engagements in England, without any present engagement of mind as to a future visit to the Coast ; yet I trust with a feeling as much disposed as ever to be resigned to such a visit if required, and not in anywise to desire to chuse my own path, but only seek to know the Divine Will concerning me in this cause, and to be enabled to do it.

May I be taught on returning home to keep in mind what I have seen and felt of the uncertain tenure of all human things, and to feel and act always as an immortal being, placed here only for a season in a state of probation, with an Eternal inheritance in view, if through Redeeming mercy I may be favoured to attain to it.

I am, with affectionate esteem,

Your friend,

HANNAH KILHAM.

Tottenham, 5th mo. 26th, 1828.

THE

CLAIMS OF WEST AFRICA

TO

𝔈𝔥𝔯𝔦𝔰𝔱𝔦𝔞𝔫 𝔍𝔫𝔰𝔱𝔯𝔲𝔠𝔱𝔦𝔬𝔫,

THROUGH

THE NATIVE LANGUAGES.

BY

HANNAH KILHAM.

LONDON:

HARVEY AND DARTON, GRACEHURCH STREET.

———

MDCCCXXX.

CLAIMS OF WEST AFRICA,

&c.

THE colony of Sierra Leone, interesting and important as it is, when regarded as a station
inhabited by Africans from more than thirty different tribes, has not yet, it must be allowed,
exhibited all those encouraging marks of advancement, either in civil or religious knowledge,
which have been anxiously desired, and which
indeed are still hoped for by many who look to
this colony as a point from which, through the
favour of Divine Goodness, may one day be extended the blessings of civilization and Christian
instruction to many nations on the wide and
almost unexplored continent of Africa.

This station having been formed and main-
tained on a principle of benevolent concern for
the good of Africa, and as a place of reception
for the unhappy victims of cruelty and oppres-

B

sion, when rescued from the slave-ships, presents a very peculiar and a very powerful claim to our interest and regard ; and the enquiry ought to be fairly met as to what really is its present state, and what the impediments to its more rapid advancement.

If from feelings of individual compassion a Christian philanthropist had rescued from the hold of a slave-ship one helpless child, and placed it under care for shelter and instruction, would he not feel so much interest for his rescued charge, as fully to inform himself from time to time how the child was cared for and instructed?— whether its physical wants as to food, shelter, and medical care were suitably provided for, and its mind receiving the advantages of appropriate instruction and judicious Christian care?

But have the advocates of the African cause as yet obtained all the information of the state of the liberated slaves, the children, and the people, when landed in Sierra Leone, which their dependent position in society has called for?—the children especially, who from their greater helplessness do assuredly claim much of a parent's care from the friends of Africa in this country? And is it not much to be desired, that regular reports should be furnished as to the manner in which these children are disposed of on arrival in the colony, and how they are subsequently provided

and cared for; how lodged, and fed, and taught?
Whether means are provided for maintaining their
health, or restoring them when sick, and for promoting their effectual instruction and improvement? Although much has been done for the
colony of Sierra Leone by the friendly care and
liberal aid of Government, and many lives have
been sacrificed in exhausting labour, by devoted
agents of the Missionary Societies, the colony is
yet, it must be allowed, but in a state of infancy,
both as respects its civil and religious advancement: at the same time, the limited state of the
population as to numbers, is such as loudly to call
for enquiry into the cause, when it is considered
how many have been brought in, from year to
year, from the captured slave-vessels.

With regard to many of the apprenticed children, there is very great reason for anxious fear
as to what becomes of them; little or no notice
being taken of them officially after they have
been put out. It is well known, that many of
the poor natives who take them as apprentices,
imagine that the money which they pay for the
indenture, constitutes a kind of purchase of the
child, and that they are then at liberty to do with
him or her whatever they please. There is
ground to fear that not a few are by some means
taken away from the colony, and again made victims of the horrid trade in human beings.

That there is a great, a distressing mortality
among the children, is, to those who make a little enquiry in the colony, a painfully conspicuous
fact; yet the *extent* of that mortality there does
not appear to exist, in any printed reports, the
means of ascertaining. We do not learn, either
with regard to the children placed out as apprentices, or in the schools, how many have
lived, and how many have died. Neither are we
informed how many in the schools *can read*, and
how many know English so far as to *understand*
what they read.

And with regard to education, from what has
been observed of African capacity, when intelligible means of instruction are given, it appears
very evident, that were suitable measures adopted
to prepare for them the elements of instruction,
in a clear and simple form, these children would
be far from being backward, either in applying to
the acquisition of useful knowledge, or in im-
bibing what they are taught. But in the system
hitherto pursued in the schools, of using English
lessons only, for children, to whom English is
quite a foreign language, (excepting that they
have a very few words in occasional and collo-
quial use,) whilst the native languages, for conversation, are of course in general use among
themselves, can it be expected that the lessons
thus learned should prove any more than mere

sound to the pupil? What would be the consequence, if we gave to an English child, at home, a Latin book to learn without any English translation, and just taught it to spell and read the Latin words? Would the child, by practising in this way acquire a knowledge of that language? Assuredly not : and it would be very unjust to complain of the want of capacity in the Africans in Sierra Leone, as the cause of their not having advanced more than they have, when that which has been offered to them as a medium of school instruction, must have been to them quite as unintelligible as a French, or Latin, or German book, without translation, would be to an English child.

For more than a century a prepossession was indulged in Great Britain, for teaching the English language to Gaelic children, by English books alone ; and the children were thus taught to read the English Scriptures, and to repeat English catechisms : and they did this ; and, so far as sound could satisfy, they appeared to be well advanced ; but they conversed constantly in the Gaelic, and were unable to give any account of what they had so freely read and repeated in English.

Eventually their directors found out their mistake, and now the Gaelic children, as well as the Welch and some of the native Irish, receive more effectual instruction in English through the medium of their own native languages.

And even with regard to the adult population, the public instruction given to the liberated Africans cannot be expected, under present circumstances, to contribute greatly to their improvement, since they are so much strangers to the English language, and have not the medium of their own languages in use, through which they might receive instruction. Let the friends of Africa be only willing to meet this difficulty, and provide means for its removal, by opening the doors for intelligible communication with the people, through the Native languages, and it will soon be discovered that Africans have powers to cultivate, and dispositions to improve, that would well repay the Christian labours of their European brethren. And let it be remembered, that as immortal and responsible beings, and equally with ourselves dependent on Redeeming power and love, they claim our sympathy and our Christian care.

It is not only for the welfare and advancement of the Africans in Sierra Leone, that we are called upon to do what we can for the improvement of the people of that colony, and for the attainment of an intelligible medium of instruction for themselves and for their children; we have also to take into view the prospective, yet deeply interesting object of preparing, through the various languages now spoken in Sierra Leone, the means of Christian instruction to many nations of Africa at a distance from that colony, whose minds we cannot hope to reach but through such a medium. With an object of so deep interest before us, what a field does Sierra Leone present! Surely the cultivation of this field, to as great an extent as circumstances are now calling for, is a Christian duty that cannot be withheld.

The work of translation into a great number of unwritten languages, must indeed be an engagement of close mental labour and of anxious responsibility. It is well known, that one great hindrance to the prosecution of such a work in Africa, is the relaxing effect of the climate on European constitutions. It must yet be allowed, that Sierra Leone, from its peculiar circumstances, in being a centre for the reception of people from so many nations, does undoubtedly afford scope for much being done there, could agents be found prepared for the work, and capable of bearing the difficulties of the climate. The time may come, when Africans themselves may *carry on* this work, if the means could now be found of giving to some of the most intelligent and well-disposed among them. such education as to prepare them for it, and at the same time establishing, through European agency, such elementary principles and introductory arrangements in the concern, as the present circumstances of the colony are calling for.

In order to raise a native agency to assist in the important and responsible work of African translations, it would be requisite that the best opportunities be afforded for the natives introduced to this work, to gain a knowledge of the English language, from whence both elementary books and Scripture lessons would have to be translated, previously to the more extensive engagement of their assisting in the translations of the Scriptures at large.

England would, no doubt, afford the best opportunities for the natives of Africa to obtain a knowledge of our language, and England would also afford the means for a strict revisal and examination of translations attempted, were intelligent natives here to give the required evidence. When the awfulness of the work of Scripture translation is considered, it must indeed be felt that every advantage of examination and revisal is greatly to be desired.

But, alas for poor Africa! how little has yet been done for that wide continent, with its thousands of peopled towns and villages: how little is yet known there of the great and important work of Scripture translations, or of the widely extended

labours of the British and Foreign Bible Society,
the rivers and streams of whose Christian bounty
have so richly flowed, even far and near, in every
other quarter of the habitable world. Oh! that
the powerful appeal of those who sit in " the
dark places of the earth," surrounded by " habi-
tations of cruelty," might be heard and regarded.
" Are we not the children of one Father?" Why
then should difficulties deter those whom Divine
Providence has favoured with many spiritual
and temporal blessings, from coming forward
in devotedness of heart in the Redeemer's
cause, to the help of this benighted and afflicted
people?

Were some who feel deeply in this cause to
come forward and contribute their part in dili-
gent Christian labour, and others to sacrifice a
portion of property, and thought, and care, much
might, through the blessing of Divine Goodness,
be speedily effected. And although an uncertainty must be incurred, as to whether natives
engaged as assistants in translation would themselves become sincere Christians, or be negli-
gent and regardless of the advantages presented to them; yet experience has proved, that
even where native agents themselves lose, by
their own subsequent misconduct, the privileges
which they might have enjoyed, the benefit of
the translations is still felt by others, and the

advantage of thus employing the tranlators is far from being lost.

It is true, indeed, that since the Church Missionary Society have now lately commenced, among their own agents, African translations, much good may be hoped from this work being carried on by them in Sierra Leone, should the lives of the individuals, to whom the work has been committed in that colony, be long continued. Yet it is well known, that their benevolent Christian interest in this cause would lead them greatly to rejoice in every facility for the promotion of the work, and they would hear gladly of the adoption of measures for its being carried forward extensively, both in Africa and in England.

Were a few well-chosen Africans to be brought, on their own desire, to this country, from some of the principal tribes, so selected as to retain their languages by conversing with each other, they might, in an Institution prepared here for their reception, rapidly acquire the English language and become valuable assistants in translation ; and preserving the general forms and structure of their own languages, these translations, written from their dictation by their English friends appointed to the work, would, if well attended to, be found clear and intelligible when heard or read in the native districts. Europeans engaged in the translation, might at the same time acquire sufficient knowledge of these languages, to check or prevent the passing of erroneous translations respecting important truths.

African agents thus trained and employed, might some of them, it is hoped, in a future day, whilst in England, give valuable help in the translation of the Scriptures; whilst others, having spent two or three years in this country, and given their assistance in translating merely elementary lessons, might return, prepared to pursue with respectability some other engagement in the colony from whence they came: yet all persons thus received into the Institution, to have the opportunity, on returning home, of continued communications with their friends here, by occasional correspondence, so long as their conduct should be such as to leave the way open for such communication.

Should encouragement be given for the prosecution of this work, it would, in present circumstances, it is hoped, be easy to obtain a good selection of pupils, who would gladly come over for a few years to learn our language, and to assist in translations in some of the principal languages of Africa. Already has the advantage of such translations been experienced in a school on the river Gambia, in which the Jolof elementary and Scripture lessons are now used, which a few years ago were prepared and printed in England under the sanction of a Committee of Friends for promoting African Instruction. These lessons have not only been used in schools for teaching the Jolof children both their own language and the English, but some of the young men have also read the Jolof Scripture lessons contained in them to their families at home. From that station are lately received accounts truly consoling and encouraging to perseverance in this labour of love.* The present Missionary in the Gambia, who has also conducted the public instruction through the medium of native interpreters, has been favoured with so much success as to induce the hope, that ere long the Native Teachers may supply that district alone, or at least without the constant residence of European missionaries.†

* See Wesleyan Missionary Notices, dated June, 1830.

† Since this appeal was put to press, the Committee of the Wesleyan Missionary Society have received the mournful intelligence, that their much esteemed and valued Missionary, Richard Marshall, who had laboured with such encouraging success in this station, during most of the last two years, died of fever after a sickness of five days, during the present rainy season. His estimable widow, with her infant child, arrived in Bristol on the 1st of 10th month : they also had been sick of fever, and ordered by their medical attendant to return to England, as the only hope, humanly speaking, of their lives being preserved. A. M. appeared, on her arrival, much restored, and gave a very satisfactory account of the state of the mission in the Gambia. Her friends, who knew and justly loved her, have since received the very unexpected and affecting intelligence, that two days after her arrival she was suddenly called away from this state of mortality.

At the same time, from the villages of liberated Africans in Sierra Leone, we hear perpetually, in the printed statements, the report of discouragement and complaint. The people understand but little of the instructions offered, and the children in the schools are under similar disadvantages. Still there is sounded among some in that colony, the alarm of a supposed impossibility of giving any other instruction than through the English language only; the languages of the natives being so many and so little known. Allowing, that so far as the residence in an English colony is intended, it is indeed desirable that the English should be known as a *general* language among the people, and be their common medium of communication; still, in the attainment even of this object, we shall find, that to cultivate, to a certain extent, each of the distinctly ascertained native languages spoken in the colony, would be the most facile and effectual means of teaching the natives English. But if the English language itself be *not understood* by the Africans, how can it be the *medium* of instruction either in their religious assemblies or in their schools? What foreigner, either German, French, or African, can teach the English but through his own vernacular language, unless it be just so much as can be gained by signs, as in teaching the deaf and dumb? This system of teaching only by signs and motions, even if desired, could not easily be practised in Africa, where all engagements requiring much thought and application are, on account of the relaxing influence of the climate, so peculiarly difficult to Europeans. Let the friends of African education then avail themselves, in teaching English, of the advantages of the simplest and most effectual system of instruction, that of *teaching through the medium of something already known to the pupil*, and acquiring at least the elements of English, through the familiar means of introductory lessons in the native languages, with the English attached to them.

In the attempt to reduce a new language to writing, it is undoubtedly requisite to use great care in every step of a work so responsible, and especially in attemping to convey in such language any religious truth : still, by close attention and repeated examination of what is prepared, it is possible to obtain clear and intelligible translations even of Scripture lessons; translations which may be clearly understood by the natives who read them. From Scripture lessons, if thus gained in each principal language, and read occasionally among the people by whom they were understood, might not we hope that even a few words thus conveyed, would avail more for their real instruction than ten thousand words spoken to them in an unknown tongue ?

The elementary works printed by the Society of Friends within the last few years, in the African languages, are the following :—

1. African Lessons, Jolof* (or Wolof) and English, in three parts. Part I. Early Lessons and easy Narratives. II. Small vocabulary, Family Advices, and Examples in Sentences on the different Parts of Speech. III. Scripture Lessons in twenty-two sections.

2. A little sketch of elementary words in Mandingo, intended as General Spelling Lessons for any of the liberated Africans or others, in a school consisting of children of different tribes, which being in the same simple orthography used in each of the present translations, would be suitable to be used by the pupils in a mixed school. The children may afterwards learn from books, each in their own language, written in the same orthography. In addition to this, a book of words and sentences on each part of speech, in the Mandingo language, together with the English, having also a few passages of Scripture in Mandingo and English. These Lessons were prepared, with the assistance

* The natives, though they call themselves Jolofs, use the term Wolof in speaking of their language.

of one of the native pupils in England, previously to the time in which several Friends went out to the Gambia, in 1823, where they were revised. (The African Lessons, Jolof and English, were also prepared in England and revised in Africa at that time.) The Mandingo tract includes the General Spelling Lessons already noticed. The charge of printing this tract was defrayed by the Committee of the Language Institution in 1827.

3. Specimens of African Languages. A book containing a short outline of words, together with the ten numbers in thirty different languages spoken in the colony of Sierra Leone, and designed for use in some of the liberated African schools. By the use of these little sketches it has been ascertained what were the native countries of several Africans in England, of different tribes long absent from their own land, and incapable of giving any further account to ascertain the districts in which they were born, excepting from their words used in numbering, and a few obvious terms in their native languages.

4. Single Lessons in the Thirty Languages: two duodecimo pages only in each. These Lessons are the same with the last, only arranged in a different form, having each language detached, and some additional words in each more than are introduced in the "Specimens." Both these Single Lessons and the Specimens are designed as a little

introduction to English, and the writer hopes, should life be given, to see the proposed system of instruction in a few months brought into practice, with the assistance of these books, in some of the liberated African schools. The materials for these lessons were prepared during the writer's last visit to Sierra Leone, excepting a few of them, which were previously obtained, and at that time revised.

5. A school book of Jolof only, containing easy lessons on subjects exhibited in twelve pictures. These lessons are printed in a twelve page tract, as the least expensive form. The Jolof schools have also the same lessons in English, and one set of pictures will serve for both.

6. A single sheet lesson, containing the alphabets ; a number of small pictures of common objects, with the native names attached : also the ten numbers in figures and words. This introductory lesson is printed in six languages each, on a separate sheet—the Mandingo, Jolof, Aku, or E-i-o, Bassa, Ibo, and Kru. A lesson of the same kind is also printed on a separate sheet in English.

There are also prepared, in addition to the printed books, a few Scripture translations in Mandingo, which are still in manuscript, and wait an opportunity for revision in Africa. A sketch of the grammar of the Jolof language in manuscript.

and a Jolof vocabulary, larger than that introduced in the printed lessons. Also a few lessons in the Sussu, obtained from a native of that country when in England, in 1829. The system pursued in the formation of these elementary lessons, or in writing African words from the voice of a native, is the following.

1st. To use only such letters as are sounded in the words, and not any mute or superfluous letters.

2nd. That each letter should express one sound only; that is, not to have the same letters used as in English for hard and soft sounds, (the *g* always hard.)

3rd. To adopt the continental sounds of the vowels, *a, e, i, o, u*, as heard in *ark, great, field, hope, truth.* The vowels to be sounded short in the beginning, or the middle of a word or syllable, and long at the end : or when required to be sounded long in the beginning or middle of a syllable, to place a dash (-) over the vowel to show the long sound.

4th. To reject the letters *c, q,* and *x*, these sounds being provided in the letters *s* and *k*.

5th. To use the compound vowel sound of *ai* for the English sound *i*, and the letters *iu* for the English sound of *u*.

6th. When a guttural sound is to be described,

to adopt the letter nearest to it, as *h* or *k*, and by the addition of a mark over the $\bar{h}$ or $\bar{k}$ to describe that sound.

This system is so simple in practice, that if adhered to, there is but little liability to write in a way that would not be easily read.

A satisfactory degree of correctness may be attained in translation, if care be only taken clearly to ascertain the first steps in the work; as by writing down from the voice of a native, the names of *visible objects*, as man, boy, &c. which are either present in the room, or the pictures of them present. Afterwards, *visible actions;* as walk, run, and so on : next, *obvious qualities*, added to some of the nouns; as a round table, a little bird ; and thus to proceed taking down different classes of words and short sentences, until by degrees not only a considerable stock of words may be obtained, but a sufficient number of

It is necessary, in obtaining some of the parts of speech, and their variations, to give a sentence in several different forms for translation, so as to ascertain perhaps an adverb, a preposition, &c. as " he walks *slowly*," " he walks *quickly*,"

" I go *to* the door," "I come *from* the door," " my
house," "my father's house;" and to analyse, with
close attention, the different parts of the simplest
sentence, carefully separating word from word.
Still, in the very first attempts, it will often be
best to leave, at least in manuscript, the pronoun
attached to the verb; as, " I go;" since the natives
will understand this better than the more abstract
terms of, "go," or " to go," (the same difficulty
they might find also in other verbs, in the terms
of the infinitive mood;) and especially to wait
with patience, and give repeated trials before we
conclude upon the correctness of terms given to
us relative to mind; as, " hope," " fear,"
" love," &c.

The very great responsibility attaching to that
part of the work of translation with which Christian instruction is connected, renders it a very desirable measure that persons so engaged should
have near to them every aid that could be obtained for the revision of their essays, by a Committee well acquainted with the general principles of
language, and prepared to give occasional help
and counsel as to any points on which there
might be more than common obscurity, or liability
to mistake. Such a Committee would, no doubt,
be without difficulty appointed, if an Institution
for translations were formed in England.

Let not any turn away from this important

subject, fearing that it is too difficult for accomplishment, or that the means of its pursuance may be inadequate and soon fail. There are certain simple principles for the prosecution of this work, which are allowed and understood by not a very few persons, and are regarded as being solid and worthy to be acted upon. May the important object of endeavouring, should Divine Providence permit, to raise up an African agency to assist in preparing the means of intelligible instruction, in an Institution for translations in England—may this important object be freely sanctioned by the friends of Africa, and perseveringly pursued, trusting in Him who can at His pleasure raise up and preserve agents for carrying on His own beneficent designs on the earth, and who has again and again evinced that it is His Divine will to carry on HIS OWN designs by instrumental agency! May it be ours to attain to a sincere desire to know and to do His will, trusting for help in Him!

Although fully aware that Friends in encouraging the work of elementary translations, so far as has been alluded to, have regarded the concern as a part of a common cause, in which, if good could be done, their attention was called for, for the sake of the cause itself; it would yet be ungrateful not to acknowledge the obligation which indeed the writer sensibly feels towards Friends

who have so kindly given every facility for the
prosecution of this work, not only in taking
charge, for several years, of the two native
Africans who assisted in the first translation,
(that of the lessons now used in the Gambia,)
but in every subsequent step, providing the requisite expences for promoting the design, and
facilitating with the most friendly confidence and
aid its further prosecution.

The obligations of the writer to a few endeared
friends in particular, must ever be combined with
the remembrance of the earliest, and every subsequent step which has been taken in this
deeply interesting cause—a cause which they
have most kindly and essentially promoted by
their judgment, by their literary aid and counsel,
by the unremitting kindnesses of Christian sympathy and hospitality, and in various other ways
in which liberal help could be given in the fur-
therance of an arduous and responsible engagement—an engagement, the difficulties of which
are not worthy to be considered, when so much
lessened by the sympathy and aid of Christian
kindness, and accompanied as they have been by
the sustaining belief that the pursuance of this
cause is in consonance with the will of the Most
High, and the feeling, that in His will alone we
find our rest.

Although the work of translation may not in

itself have all the attraction of some other engagements, yet its ultimate object, when directed to
the attainment, for a suffering and benighted
people, of that divine revelation in the Scriptures
of Truth, with which we have ourselves been so
mercifully favoured, the prospect of this attainment may well give a deep and lasting interest to
long-continued exertions in such a cause—an
interest which will live, and grow, and still ex-
pand, when occupations that need the zest of
novelty for their support shall cease to excite
their wonted attraction.

It should never be forgotten, that Translations
are as indispensably requisite to the cause of
Christian education in heathen lands, as Schools
are necessary to the effectual diffusion of the
Holy Scriptures. We must be satisfied to com-
mence with the earliest steps, and should surely
feel great thankfulness for the favour of being
permitted to take any step in a cause so precious
as that of preparing, in the least degree, to open
the way for our African brethren to a knowledge
of those sacred records which direct to " Him of
whom Moses and the prophets wrote."

With an object in view so important and so
delightful to every feeling of Christian love, it is
therefore proposed, that a few, to whom the advancement of truth and righteousness on the
earth is precious, should, without further delay

make arrangements for the introduction of a few
native Africans into this country, selected from
some of the most important tribes known in the
colony of Sierra Leone, or other parts of West
Africa, as Mandingo, Jolof, Bassa, &c. and
brought over with their own concurrence and
desire, to be taught here the English language,
and prepared to give assistance in translating
from the English into their own languages.

2nd. That after appointing a Provisional Committee for carrying this design into effect, arrangements be made for providing the requisite funds,
and for directing the means by which Africans
shall be selected, and introduced to the proposed
means of instruction.

3rd. That at a suitable time a house be hired
for the purpose, and care taken to have it sufficiently warm to shield the natives of a hot climate from the dangers they would otherwise be
exposed to during the winter season.

4th. That persons be engaged to take the
charge of the family as to domestic care, School
instruction, and the prosecution of Translations.

6th. That the Committee take the charge, as
far as may be found expedient, of printing, in
different languages, Elementary books and Scripture lessons.

Any persons disposed to give their sanction

and aid to the proposed object, by Subscription
or Donations, are requested to give notice of thei
purpose, or to forward their Contributions t
DREWETT and FOWLER, 60, Old Broad Street, o
to any of the following Friends, who have agree
to act as a Committee to carry the preceding
plan into effect, provided they meet with th
requisite pecuniary support.

> WILLIAM ALLEN,
> JOHN THOMAS BARRY,
> PETER BEDFORD,
> JOHN CAPPER,
> SAMUEL DARTON,
> JOSIAH FORSTER,
> ROBERT FORSTER,
> WILLIAM HARGRAVE,
> THOMAS HODGKIN, M. D.
> WM. FORSTER REYNOLDS,
> JOHN SANDERSON.

*Extract of a Letter from an experienced and
devoted Agent of the Church Missionary
Society, who is now engaged in the work of
African Translations, dated Sept.* 19, 1828.

" The observations contained in your communication on the advantage of preparing elementary books in this country, in preference to
Africa, meet my entire concurrence.   The more
I reflect on the subject the more I see the very
great importance of studying the native languages in every point of view ; but especially, as
you remark, when connected with the great and
and blessed object of advancing the cause of our
Redeemer.

" Of the dangers to which Africans, especially
young persons, are exposed when brought to this
country for instruction, I am fully sensible.   I
trust, however, it may be found, that with proper attention to situation and management, they
are not wholly insurmountable.

" With respect to the great difficulty of sustaining the mental exertion necessary in the
study of languages, while resident in Africa, I
can speak in some measure from experience.
It appears to me next to impossible that the

work can be carried on with any thing like desirable speed, by an individual or two exposed to the debilitating effects of a tropical climate; while, in order to be performed effectively, such supervision as you suggest would, I think, be necessary. For though the *sounds* must undoubtedly be learned from natives, yet as to the manner of *expressing* those sounds, and as to the construction of any particular language, valuable assistance might probably be derived from individuals in this country who are well acquainted with language in general. So far, therefore, as I have yet considered the subject, I conceive that a work of this kind would be best carried on conjointly, in England and in Africa at the same time.

" When I reflect on the great labour required to communicate knowledge to Africans, through the medium of English, and the degree of uncertainty which exists as to the precise result of that labour, I am forcibly impressed with the very great importance of adopting another plan ; that is, of endeavouring to open the natural channel of communication between them and us, by becoming acquainted with their languages, and by reducing them to writing. Indeed, I can scarcely help wondering that such a plan should not have been more decidedly adopted. and more vigorously pursued in times past. Having, however, once more been brought forward, I hope it will never be lost sight of, till, through the blessing of the Most High upon the exertions of those who may give themselves to this work, the inestimable treasure of the Scriptures shall be laid open to all the tribes of our African brethren who are or may be within our reach.

THE END.

Harvey and Darton, Printers, Gracechurch Street.

For EU product safety concerns, contact us at Calle de José Abascal, 56–1°, 28003 Madrid, Spain or eugpsr@cambridge.org.

www.ingramcontent.com/pod-product-compliance
Ingram Content Group UK Ltd.
Pitfield, Milton Keynes, MK11 3LW, UK
UKHW012336130625
459647UK00009B/310